MW00398480

This book belongs to:

____

Made in United States
Orlando, FL
12 March 2023

30982851R00061